RECHA...

Inspirational
Insights

to Spiritual Renewal

DEVOTIONAL WRITINGS

by

B.J. Roberts

ISBN 978-1-57550-116-1

First Printing
Printed in the United States of America

CONTENTS

21-DAY
Speak Life
Challenge

RECHARGE!

Day-1

Let the words of my mouth,

and the meditation of my heart,

be acceptable in thy sight,

O Lord,

my strength,

and my redeemer.

Psalms 19:14

The purpose of the Speak Life Challenge is to make a deliberate effort to guard the negative words that come out of our mouths.

However, I couldn't get around the fact that our words are an overflow of our heart. Dealing with negative words without first dealing with our hearts is like taking a pain pill for back problems. The symptoms will reoccur until the root of the issue is fixed.

Our mouth will speak out of the abundance of our heart. What we say is an indication of what is in us. We speak negative words because our thoughts are negative.

Proverbs 4:23 says to *"Guard your heart with all diligence for out of it are the issues of LIFE."* We guard our words by guarding our hearts.

Pay attention to the negative things you may get ready to say, such as "I can't stand this," "They get on my nerves," and "This is stupid." Check your heart to see why you are saying it.

Today's confession

is from Psalm 51:10.

Every time you get ready to

speak something negative,

make this confession:

"Create in me a clean heart, O God

and renew a right spirit in me."

Let the Challenge begin!

Day-2

This book of the law

shall not depart out of thy mouth;

but thou shalt meditate therein day and night,

that thou mayest observe to do according to

all that is written therein:

for then thou shalt make thy way prosperous,

and then thou shalt have

good success.

Joshua 1:8

Day 1 of the Challenge dealt with guarding our hearts in Proverbs 4:23. The use of the word hearts in that scripture ultimately deals with our thoughts. Our thoughts have to do with what is in our mind.

Guarding our hearts is the first step to the renewing of our minds. Romans 12:2 says to *"Be transformed by the renewing of our minds."*

Renewing is the same thing as renovating a house. A house renewal begins by getting rid of the old before you begin putting in the new.

The final product is a transformation of the house.

Spiritually speaking, transformation comes through renovation; renovation is a result of meditation. Meditation is not a new age idea of positive thinking. It is a biblical concept of focusing our thoughts on God's Word and speaking what His word says. Our thoughts will naturally turn away from the negative and toxic strongholds in our minds as we turn our focus toward God and His Word.

Quit focusing on the negative and what you can't do. Instead, focus on the promises in God's word and what you can do. Believe in your heart, confess with your mouth, and your way will be prosperous and you will have good success.

Today's confession for any negativity

that may arise is:

"I am being transformed

by the Word of God.

I will have good success."

Day-3

Who hath believed our report?

and to whom is the arm

of the Lord revealed?

Isaiah 53:1

Days 1 and 2 of the Challenge dealt with the condition of our heart and thoughts.

Why? Because the process to speaking life begins within. 2 Corinthians 10:4-5 talks about strongholds and our thoughts. Strongholds are a sustained collection of thoughts that eventually turn into our belief system. Strongholds from the enemy are always composed of lies because the devil is a liar. These thought collections begin to influence our faith and how we live. Faith is conviction and conviction is a firm persuasion. Paul, the Apostle, said he was fully persuaded in whom he believed.

According to Hebrews 10:23, our profession is a profession of faith. We believe and we speak.

Strongholds will tell you that "You can't, you've messed up too badly, you'll never be free, you'll always be sick."

The devil is a liar! I want to encourage you to put on the mind of Christ and break free from the lies of the enemy.

Believe the report of the Lord. His report is recorded in Isaiah 53:4-5 *"Surely He hath borne our griefs and carried our sorrows: yet we did esteem Him stricken, smitten of God, and afflicted. But He was wounded for our transgressions, He was bruised for our iniquities: the chastisement of our peace was upon Him; and with His stripes we are healed."*

Today's confession is:

"I am healed, free,

and forgiven

by the blood of Jesus."

Day-4

We have the same spirit of faith,

according as it is written,

I believed,

and therefore have I spoken;

we also believe,

and therefore speak.

2 Corinthians 4:13

Faith is confidence. Faith is assurance. Faith is belief in an invisible God who is able to do tangible things is your life. Faith is a spirit.

Doubt and unbelief are spirits too. In many cases, doubt and unbelief will work through self-condemnation and false humility.

1 John 3:21 says *"Beloved, if our heart condemn us not, then have we confidence toward God."*

False humility and condemnation will tell you that you're not worthy to receive the goodness of God. However, once you are cleansed by the blood, it's no longer about your worthiness or goodness. It is about His.

9

2 Corinthians 5:21 tells us that you are now the righteousness of God in Christ. Your profession comes from your position. You are seated in heavenly places in Christ. You are the Redeemed of the Lord. Let the Redeemed of the Lord say so. Let a spirit of faith arise in you today and take the authority you have been given.

Today's confession is:

"I am the Righteousness of God

in Christ Jesus."

Day-5

His divine power has granted to us all
things that pertain to life and godliness,
through the knowledge of Him who
called us to His own glory and
excellence, by which He has granted to
us His precious and very great
promises, so that through them you
may become partakers of the divine na-
ture, having escaped from the
corruption that is in the world
because of sinful desire.

2 Peter 1:3-4

This passage of scripture is loaded with promises for those who have surrendered their lives
to Jesus. The Christ life is no longer forced to
live in the natural but the supernatural. You
have been given His divine nature. His divine
power has given you everything you need for
life and godliness.

You have been called to His glory and excellence. Mediocrity is not an option. Defeat is not an option. Failure is not an option. God's got your back and is on your side. The thief comes to steal, kill, and destroy but Jesus came to give life more abundantly.

Abundant life is yours. He has given you great and precious promises. You don't have to work for them. They're given. Receive it by faith. Believe it. Speak it. See it.

Today's confession is:

"I have abundant life

and walk in the promises

of God"

Day-6

But he said to me,
'My grace is sufficient for you,
for my power is made perfect
in weakness.'
Therefore, I will boast
all the more gladly
of my weaknesses,
so that the power of Christ
may rest upon me.

2 Corinthians 12:9

Weakness, by definition, is a lack of strength in the body, of the soul, or of understanding.

Every person alive has struggled with weakness in one form or another. Some are dealing with weakness in your body, some with weakness in your emotions, others are dealing with a lack of understanding.

You must not look at weakness in terms of failure. Rather, look at weakness as an opportunity for a miracle. Miracles start where human strength and ability ends. Your place of weakness is where God releases His grace and perfects His power.

Do you feel weak right now? If so, you are a candidate for a miracle.

Joel 3:10 says "...*let the weak say, I am strong.*" I pray God gives you supernatural strength and cover you with grace.

Today's confession is:

"I am strong.

I have the power of God working in my life."

Day-7

Trust in the Lord with all thine heart;
and lean not unto thine own understanding.
In all thy ways acknowledge Him,
and He shall direct thy paths.

Proverbs 3:5-6

Trusting the Lord is a vital ingredient to our walk with Him.

Why? Because many times we may walk through circumstances or situations we may not understand but have to trust that God will direct our path.

There is a difference made between trusting God and trusting ourselves. Leaning to our understanding will always cause us to live in a place where we are 'standing under' the promises of God for our lives.

King David walked through many difficult situations but still wrote in Psalm 20:7 *"Some trust in chariots and some in horses: but we will remember the name of the Lord our God."*

15

Psalm 37:5 says *"Commit your way to the Lord: trust in Him and He will act."*

Today's confession is

"I trust you Lord.

My way is established

and You are acting on my behalf."

Day-8

And David was greatly distressed;

for the people spake of stoning him,

because the soul of all the people was grieved,

every man for his sons and for his daughters:

but David encouraged himself

in the Lord his God.

1 Samuel 30:6

Some of the most uplifting and inspiring verses recorded in the Bible are in the book of Psalms and recorded from the mouth of David.

In spite of fierce opposition, many trials, and even attempts to take his life, David remained steadfast and trusted in the Lord's ability to see him through. The great thing about David is he knew how to encourage himself in the Lord.

You can't always rely on others. Sometimes you just have to know that you and God make

17

a majority and if God is for you, who can be against you?

Encourage yourself. Declare the goodness and favor of God over your life. Declare the healing and miracle working power of God over yourself.

Psalm 18:2 says *"The Lord is my Rock, and my fortress, and my deliverer, my God, my strength, in whom I will trust, my Shield, and the horn of my salvation, my Stronghold."*

Today's confession is:

"God is for me.

Who can be against me?"

Be encouraged.

Speak Life

Day-9

For You equipped me

with strength for the battle.

Psalm 18:39

Are you in a battle? Does it feel like you are in the fight of your life?

Maybe you are in a battle for your family, health, finances, or your faith. As a Christian, battles are inevitable. It's not a question of whether or not you will have any battles but how you will fight them. We must not fight in the natural but in the spiritual.

1 Timothy 6:12 says that it is a faith fight. Our weapons are not fleshly but mighty through God to the pulling down of strongholds.

There are several things to remember while in the battle.

1 - You are already on the winning side.

2 - The devil knows you are on the winning side, so don't believe his lies.

3 - Use your weapons.

19

Ephesians 6:17 says we have the sword of the Spirit which is the Word of God. The Word of God is the Holy Spirit's sword.

My encouragement to you is start swinging your sword. Get a Word from God and fight.

Today's confession is

"I have strength for the battle

and I WILL win!"

Day-10

While we look not

at the things which are seen,

but at the things which are not seen:

for the things which are seen

are temporal;

but the things which are not seen

are eternal.

2 Corinthians 4:18

Where has your focus been? What preoccupies your thoughts and emotions - the temporal things or the eternal things?

We must pray for discernment to see ourselves and our situations through eyes of faith. Faith sees the invisible, believes the impossible, expects the unimaginable. Faith is eternal.

What we see is temporal or temporary, which means it can and will change. Never allow a temporary situation to take authority over your eternal revelation.

Here's a paraphrase of 2 Corinthians 4:8-9, "We are surrounded by trouble but too blessed to be stressed. We are perplexed but have not given up hope. Persecuted, but God has not forsaken us. We've been knocked down but have not been knocked out."

Paul, the apostle could write this because he was looking at the eternal, not the temporary.

Today's confession is:

"I am steadfast and will see

the Glory of God in my life."

Day-11

So shall my word be

that goeth forth out of my mouth:

it shall not return unto me void,

but it shall accomplish that which I please,

and it shall prosper in the thing

whereto I sent it.

Isaiah 55:11

A principle in biblical interpretation is the law of first mention. The law of first mention means to identify the first time a principle or concept is mentioned in the Bible and then see where else it is repeated throughout the rest of scripture.

An example of this is recorded in Genesis 1:3, *"And God said, let there be light: and there was light."*

The principle, here, is when God does something, He does so through His Word. When God wanted light, He spoke light. When God wanted the seas, He spoke the seas into existence.

When God wanted to bring salvation to mankind, He sent THE Word: Jesus.

Psalm 107:20 says, *"He sent His word, and healed them."* God's Word is powerful, life-giving, creative, and productive. His Word will prosper wherever it is sent. Sent means to order. We don't order God; but we order our situations by sending His Word.

Today's confession is:

"God's Word is working in my life."

Day-12

Thou shalt also decree a thing,

and it shall be established unto thee:

and the light shall shine

upon thy ways.

Job 22:28

Jesus taught His disciples often about prayer and challenged their faith as well.

Prayer and faith both have various levels and elements for us to learn. Many times, we view prayer as solely interrogative. We ask God questions and He gives us answers. While this is true, prayer is and should also be declarative.

Mark 11:23 tells us that whoever 'says' to the mountain, be removed. It does not say to ask God about the mountain. It says to say to the mountain.

In terms of prayer, you have to know when to pray it and when to say it. Sometimes, you have to quit praying about your mountains and start speaking to them and tell them to be removed.

Jesus has given us authority. The key part of the word authority is 'author'. Author's deal in the case of words. Jesus is the author and finisher of our faith. Our authority will be represented by our words. Decree a thing and it shall be established unto thee.

Today's confession is:

"I have authority. I speak to my mountain

and tell it to be removed in Jesus name."

Day-13

Therefore it is of faith,

that it might be

by grace.

Romans 4:16

A key ingredient to seeing the promises of God come to pass in our lives is Grace.

It's very easy to think that we can earn God's promises. However, the fact is, we are who we are and we have what we have by the grace of God.

God's grace is His unmerited favor. Unmerited means you can't work for it or be good enough to deserve it. It's Grace!

You have to know that God is a giver. It is His nature. He gets joy out of giving gifts to His children.

Grace is a gift.

Salvation is a gift.

Healing is a gift.

Deliverance is a gift.

A gift is something you just receive. Receive, by faith, God's gifts for your life.

Today's confession is:
"I declare God's grace in my life
and walk in favor."

Day-14

Jesus entered the house and said to them,

'Why are you crying

and making so much noise?

The child is not dead, only asleep.'

But they laughed at him.

So, after throwing them out of the house...

Mark 5:39-40

Jesus has entered into the house where Jairus's daughter had died. Jairus was a leader of the synagogue but came to Jesus for help.

First, recognize Jairus was a member of the religious community who would eventually deliver Jesus to the Cross, but he came to Jesus anyhow. No doubt, in spite of the opposition of his peers.

Second, when Jesus gets to the house, it is full of mourners over the child's death. The house was full of negativity. Jesus speaks words of faith in the midst of the negativity and the people laughed at Him and ridiculed His words.

Don't be surprised when people laugh at you because of your courageous declaration of faith.

Third, "so AFTER throwing them out of the house." Notice how Jesus threw the negative influences out of the house before He performed the miracle.

Throw out the negative and toxic influences; the people who try to cause you to doubt what you know God has said; the ones speaking doubt and curses over you. If your dream, ministry, vision, or hope is dead like Jairus's daughter, be like Jesus. Get the doubt out and speak life!

Today's confession is:

"My life is free from doubt.

My dreams will arise."

Day-15

Jesus Christ

the same yesterday,

and today, and forever.

Hebrews 13:8

Praise God that our faith is not defined by events or circumstances. It is not affected by the stock market or altered by new governments. It is not archaic like a history book but alive, active, and absolute.

Faith is not about "What" but "Who." It is not about things but a person, Jesus Christ.

This is important to know because your life will follow wherever you place your trust. If you trust in money, you will follow after money. If you trust in people, you will constantly follow after and seek the approval of people.

That is why we always trust in Jesus. Trust means to have an assured reliance on the character, strength, or truth of someone. We trust Him because we rely on His character, strength, and truth. He'll never let you down, never let you fall, never let you fail if you put your trust in Him.

I love to sing the old hymn:

> "Tis so sweet to trust in Jesus,
> just to take Him at His word.
> Just to rest upon His promise.
> Just to know, thus saith the Lord.
> Jesus, Jesus, how I trust Him.
> How I prove Him o'er and o'er.
> Jesus, Jesus, precious Jesus.
> Oh for Grace to trust Him more."

Today's confession is simple:

"Jesus, I believe You

and I trust You."

Day-16

(As it is written, I have made thee a father

of many nations,)

before him whom he believed,

even God, who quickeneth the dead,

and calleth those things

which be not as though they were.

Romans 4:17

In times of storms or power outages, many people rely on generators. Generators are devices that convert mechanical energy to electrical energy, such as, gasoline into electricity. They do not produce electricity but convert one form of energy into another. Just as a water pump does not produce water but rather creates a flow of water.

In the spirit realm, faith is a generator. Faith does not produce healing. Faith takes healing that already exists in the spirit and converts it to the natural.

Faith converts what is in eternity (Heaven) and causes it to manifest in time and space (earth). Faith empowers you to pray as Jesus taught, *"Thy Kingdom come, Thy will be done, in earth as it is in heaven."*

Your healing already exists and faith will generate your healing in the natural. This causes you to call the things that do not exist as though they already did.

Prayer is a key to the kingdom, but faith turns the key and unlocks the door. There is no sickness, depression, or bondage in heaven. Use your faith to generate what is in heaven down to earth.

You will have to tailor-make your own confession today, but here's a start –

"I call myself healed.

I call myself delivered.

I call myself blessed."

Call the things that be not

as though they were.

Day-17

Nay, in all these things

we are more than conquerors

through him that loved us.

Romans 8:37

As believers, we need to recognize the source of our victory. Victory is a mindset, a way of thinking and living.

Our victory is not something that is going to be won in the future. It has already been won by our Savior through His death, burial, and resurrection. Jesus has already defeated the powers of darkness.

Colossians 2:15 says that Jesus spoiled principalities and powers and made a shew of them openly. In other words, Jesus made a trophy out of the devil. He defeated death, hell, and the grave; rose on the third day with all power; and forever reigns as King of Kings and Lord of Lords. There is no force in hell that can stand up to His power. There is no demon or force of darkness that can compare to His ma-

35

jestic light and splendor. He is the victorious conqueror!

Romans 8:37 says that we are MORE than conquerors. How can we be more than conquerors? Because Jesus won the battle for us and gave us HIS victory. Our job is to know Him for who He is, know who we are in Him, and know who He is in us. Then we begin to use the faith that He gave us to enforce the victory that He won.

"This is the victory that overcomes the world; even our faith." (1 John 5:4)

Today's confession comes from

2 Corinthians 2:14

"Now thanks be unto God,

which always causes us to triumph

in Christ."

Day-18

Through faith we understand that
the worlds were framed by the word of God,
so that things which are seen were not made of
things which do appear.

Hebrews 11:3

Think about a picture that you have hanging on a wall. Chances are, you can describe the picture in detail. Now think about the frame. We tend to forget that the frame plays a factor to the picture being on the wall. Without the frame, the picture would begin folding at the edges and would not hold its form for very long.

God's Word is just like that frame. Hebrews 1:3 says all things are upheld by the Word of His power. Notice, the word of God, what He speaks, framed the world and upholds what He framed.

Just as the Lord framed the worlds with His Word, we can frame our world by our words.

37

Proverbs 18:21 says that death and life are in the power of the tongue.

What kind of words have you been speaking and what kind of frame does the picture of your life depend upon for structure? Is the picture of your life surrounded by a frame of doubt, unbelief, sickness, depression, or poverty? Or, is the picture of your life surrounded by the same frame that framed the world? God's Word.

Make a decision today to start framing your life by the Word of the Lord.

Today's confession is:

"My life is framed and upheld

by the Word of God."

Day-19

Many are the plans

in the mind of a man,

but it is the purpose of the Lord

that will stand.

Proverbs 19:21

Providence is a rarely used word in our day and time. However, understanding providence is important to understanding faith.

Providence is defined as "divine guidance, making provision for the future, or to foresee." In God terms, providence means whatever God creates, He sees the future of that creation and takes part in the guidance and provision of His creation so that His creation will accomplish His will."

You are God's creation and He is actively working on your behalf. In spite of what others do to derail you, in spite of what the enemy may throw at you, when all is said and done, God WILL accomplish His will.

Isaiah 46:10 says He has already declared your ending from your beginning.

Psalm 37:23 tells us that He is ordering your steps.

God has not forgotten about you. You are His creation! You just have to trust Him and follow where He orders your steps.

It takes faith to follow, especially when you don't understand where He is taking you.

Walk by faith and not by sight. Rely on the providence of God and believe He is working all things out for your good.

Today's confession is:

"My steps are ordered

by the Lord

and His purpose

will prevail in my life."

Day-20

Thou wilt keep him in perfect peace,

whose mind is stayed on thee:

because he trusteth in thee.

Isaiah 26:3

Let's look at the principle of trusting in God.

The word trust is the New Testament equivalent for the word Faith. Trust means to be bold, confident, or careless.

I like to think of it as to Care-Less, which is the absence of care. This does not mean to have an "I don't care about anything" attitude. It is, however, to be free from anxiety, worry, concern, and fear.

1 Peter 5:7 says *"casting all your care upon Him, for He cares for you."* We have the privilege of a care-less life in the Lord.

Quit trying to rely upon yourself to fix everything. Self reliance tells God that I don't need Your help. It also makes the anxiety, worry, and fear your responsibility as well. Trusting God is the cure for care.

Isaiah 26:3 says *"He will keep you in perfect peace when we keep our mind focused on Him."*

The reason we keep our mind focused on Him is because we trust Him. Your mind will automatically focus on what it is trained to trust.

Purposely remind yourself of the goodness of the Lord. His grace is sufficient. He didn't save you to forsake you. He didn't redeem you to reject you.

Psalm 62:8 says *"Trust in Him at all times; you people, pour out your heart before: God is a refuge for us."*

Today's confession is:

"I am free from worry,

anxiety, and fear

because God cares for me."

Day-21

And shall not God

avenge his own elect,

which cry day and night unto him,

though he bear long with them?

Luke 18:7

Luke 18 tells the parable of a persistent widow and the unjust judge. This judge is described as not fearing God and having no respect for man. The widow kept coming to this judge for legal protection. For a while, the judge would not answer but finally gave in because of her persistence in asking. He basically said, "this lady is driving me crazy."

The judge then asks this question, "and shall not God avenge His own elect, which cry day and night to Him?" Jesus answers this question with a, YES He will.

I want to encourage you to be persistent. Persistent means to go on resolutely, firm in purpose, stubbornly, in spite of difficulties.

Sometimes you just have to be stubborn in

43

your faith. Don't change your requests based on the changing of facts. Stay persistent based on God's Word. Circumstances, situations, and difficulties will change. God's Word will not.

You are not bothering God. He commanded us in Matthew 7:7, *"Ask and keep on asking, seek and keep on seeking, knock and keep on knocking."*

Push on that situation with prayer, confession, and the power of the Holy Spirit. Pray until something happens. Be persistent. Don't give up. Feed your faith and starve your doubts.

Though the vision may tarry, wait for it. It will come to pass. He may not come when you want Him, but He's always on time. Hold on, help is on the way.

Today's confession is:

"I won't give up or give in

because my help is on the way!"

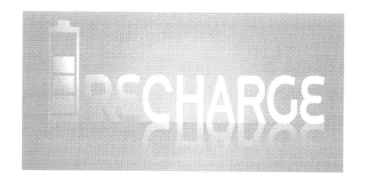

7-DAY
ELEVATE

RECHARGE!

Day 1 - DEDICATE

On this first day, we dedicate ourselves, and commit our prayers to a purpose or cause. The definition of Dedicate is to devote wholly to a purpose or cause and it comes from the Latin word meaning to Declare.

I believe how we start on day one will affect how we finish on day seven.

In 1 Samuel 17:29, David asks the question *"Is there not a cause?"* He asked this in the midst of an entire Israelite army hiding because they were afraid of one giant. David, however, was more interested in the Cause than he was concerned with the challenge. He made a decision to Dedicate himself to the cause. The cause of slaying Goliath.

After David showed his dedication, he goes on to show us his Declaration. In 1 Samuel 17:45-46, David Declares *"Then said David to the Philistine, Thou comest to me with a sword, and with a spear, and with a shield: but I come to thee in the name of the LORD of hosts, the God of the armies of Israel, whom thou hast defied. This day will the LORD deliver thee into mine hand; and I will smite thee, and take thine head from thee..."*

He made this bold declaration because he fully expected God to back it up!

I may not know what your cause is or what your Goliath is, but God does, and He wants to back you up in this fight.

Look at your giants of debt, disease, depression, and disorder and tell them 'I come to you in the Name of the Lord of hosts and God's got my back.' Dedicate and devote yourself to the cause.

Let's start out on day one with dedication and declaration. Psalm 91:2 states *"I will say of the Lord, He is my refuge and fortress: my God in Him will I trust."*

Here is your declaration for the day:

'You are my refuge, my fortress, my God:

I WILL trust YOU.'

God bless you on our journey to

ELEVATE!

Day 2 - CONSECRATE

The word for day two is Consecrate. Consecrate means to make sacred, holy, to set apart, and to sanctify.

Day one was about dedication to a cause. Dedication is a good thing, but is of little value in the Kingdom without consecration. There are a lot of people dedicated to a lot of different things but if what we are doing has not been made holy by God then we are forced to go on our own strength.

Exodus 32:29 says *"For Moses had said, Consecrate yourselves today to the LORD, even every man upon his son, and upon his brother; that he may bestow upon you a blessing this day."*

Consecration always precedes blessing. Why? Because it lines our desires up with His. This is key in producing holiness in our lives. Holiness is a by-product of consecration. We don't consecrate because we're holy. We consecrate in order to produce holiness.

Consecration was a vital ingredient for Aaron and his sons in regards to serving in the priesthood. Leviticus 8:33 says *"And ye shall not go out of the door of the tabernacle of the congregation in seven days, until the days of your consecration be at an end: for seven days shall he consecrate you.*" The priests had to consecrate for seven days which is also the number of days we are praying and fasting.

It is important to understand the priest's role in the Bible. The priests ministered TO God FOR the people. Whereas, prophets ministered TO the people FOR God.

If we will receive it, the Holy Spirit is releasing a priestly anointing upon us. This anointing will give us the supernatural ability to take the needs of the people to God.

The last point I'll make for today is Leviticus 8:33 which says "*for seven days shall HE consecrate you.*" It is the Lord who does the setting apart and making us holy. All we have to do is seek Him and He will do the rest.

Today's declaration:

I am the righteousness of God

in Christ Jesus.

Set Apart for His work.

Day 3 - ELIMINATE

The word for day three is Eliminate. Eliminate means to remove or get rid of; to reflect as being unimportant or irrelevant or to remove from consideration or competition. It comes from a Latin word which means turned out of doors. Let's look at three quick areas of ways to eliminate from the definition.

1) Remove or get rid of. Eliminate things in and around us. Hebrews 12:1 says to lay aside every weight and the sin that besets or weighs us down. What do you need to see eliminated IN you? Pray Psalm 51:10 *"Lord, create in me a clean heart and renew a right spirit within me."*

Maybe there are some people who need to be eliminated from your life. Maybe some situations need to be eliminated. MAYBE, just maybe, eliminating some people will eliminate some situations. I'm not saying to write people off forever but I am saying that you may need a season of distancing yourself in order to silence all the conflicting voices.

2) To reject as unimportant or irrelevant. Don't let your attention be consumed with unimportant things. Ask yourself, how much does this matter in comparison to eternity? Many times we find ourselves fighting battles that

don't matter in the greater plan of life. Hold your peace and let God fight your battles. There's an old saying, the squeaky wheel get the grease. I say, change the wheel. Eliminate the unimportant squeaky wheels in your life.

3) To remove from competition. Surround yourself with people that complete you, not compete with you. Colossians 2:10 says we are complete in Jesus. Let Jesus complete you. Let Jesus fill the voids and make up the deficits in your life. You are never in a competition with people when you are in a state of completion in HIM.

Today's declaration:

I am complete in You.

All weights and hindering forces

are removed from my life,

TODAY!

Day 4 - REJUVENATE

I want to focus day four on the word Rejuvenate. Rejuvenate means to restore to youthful vigor; to make fresh or new; to renew the activity of a stream by uplift or by removal of a barrier in the stream bed.

So what does that mean to you? I'm glad you asked.

1) Restore youthful vigor- Isaiah 40:31 tells us *"they that wait upon the Lord shall renew their strength."*

I found in life that sometimes you have to wait before you ELEVATE. The amazing thing about waiting in the kingdom is it makes you stronger (renews your strength). I've heard it said before whatever doesn't kill you will only make you stronger. Get ready for your strength to be rejuvenated.

2) To make fresh- Isaiah 43:19 says *"Behold, I will do a new thing; now it shall spring forth..."* 'New' in the Hebrew means fresh. I am believing for a freshness in the spirit to be released. Verse 19 even tells us when it will happen....NOW it shall spring forth. My NOW faith (Hebrew 11:1) is believing for a NOW refreshing.

3) To renew the activity of a stream by uplift or by removal of a barrier- John 7:38 *"He that believeth in me, as the scripture hath said, out of his belly shall flow rivers of living water."*

Don't be frustrated if you feel as though there is a blockage in the inside of you. The Holy Spirit is going to rejuvenate your stream.

To renew by uplift. Uplift means, Get Ready....to lift up, raise or (yep you guessed it) to ELEVATE! I didn't make that up. I got it from dictionary.com. Just declare, "It's my time to ELEVATE!"

The stream is also rejuvenated by the removal of a barrier. Praise God! Everything that has seemed to be a road block in your life will turn out to be the stepping stones the Lord uses to ELEVATE you.

Today's declaration:

I thank you Lord

that You are renewing my strength

and rejuvenating my stream.

NOW it will spring forth!

Day 5 - ANTICIPATE

I am getting excited as each day passes. Which brings me to the word for day five - Anticipate.

As usual, let's look at the definition. Anticipate means to realize beforehand; foretaste or foresee, to expect, to act in advance. Hebrews 11:1 *"Now faith is the substance of things hoped (expected/anticipated) for, the evidence of things not seen."* This could actually read "Faith is the Assurance of things Anticipated."

Faith is the supernatural ability to see what you cannot see. Anticipate means to foresee.

Read this next line a few times to get it into your spirit - You have to see it, before you see it, or you never will see it!

Psalm 34:8 says *"O taste and see that the Lord is good."* The order is taste then see. Once you get a taste of victory, you can begin to see victory again. To act in Advance.

Faith without works is dead. Acting in advance shows a belief in what you are anticipating. You clean the house when you are anticipating company. You get the nursery together when you are anticipating the arrival of a baby. The act of fasting and praying leading up to Fri-

55

day's prayer service is in anticipation of what the Lord is going to do.

Anticipating goes beyond expecting. You can be expecting a child but not do anything to prepare.

Anticipation makes preparation

for my expectation.

Put feet to your faith

and get ready for God to move.

Day 6 - ILLUMINATE

The word for day six is Illuminate. Illuminate means to brighten with light to enlighten.

Yesterday we looked at the word Anticipate. I believe that Anticipation leads to Illumination and Illumination is the key to Revelation.

Paul wrote to the church at Ephesus that *"the eyes of their understanding would be enlightened so they would KNOW..."* (Ephesians 1:18) He prayed for illumination. He knew and understood the principle revelation.

There is a big difference between information and revelation. Information helps your head. Revelation strengthens your spirit. The enemy can fool you with information; but he can't sway you once you get revelation.

Every true source of revelation comes from God's Word. Any and all illumination should always be backed by scripture. Psalm 119:105 tells us *"God's word is a lamp to our feet and a light to our path."* Following anything other than God's word will always take us off course and cause us to lose our light.

God wants to reveal Himself and His word to you. We just have to ask. Paul prayed for enlightenment and for the spirit of wisdom and revelation. (Ephesians 1:17) Ask for revelation and He will give it.

Everything God does on the earth, He does with a word. When He created the earth - He spoke a Word. (Genesis 1:-3, Hebrews 11:3) When He wanted to redeem mankind - He sent THE Word. (John 1:1) When He turns your situation around - He'll send a Word.

Pray, seek Him, and listen. He is always speaking, but sometimes we're just not listening. Ask the Lord for Illumination and Revelation today. He desires to speak to His children and I believe He will speak to you today.

Today's Declaration:

Father I thank You for giving me

the spirit of wisdom and revelation.

Holy Spirit, reveal God's word to me

in Jesus Name!

(This is the prayer I pray all the time, especially when studying)

Day 7 - ELEVATE

The word for today is - ELEVATE. The seven days have gone: Dedicate > Consecrate > Eliminate > Rejuvenate > Anticipate > Illuminate > ELEVATE!

Anticipation leads to Revelation. Revelation leads to ELEVATION. Elevate means to raise to a higher place, position, or spiritual level.

It's hard to see yourself on the mountain when you feel as though you've always been in a valley. It's difficult to see victory when you always feel defeated. But elevation in the kingdom has nothing to do with how we feel. Elevation comes through revelation. Revelation is the ability to see into the spirit realm.

To know by faith what you cannot know in the natural. It is having spiritual vision that transcends any and all circumstances, situations, or trials.

Ephesians 2:6 tells us that *"He has RAISED us up together, and made us sit together in heavenly places in Christ Jesus."*

Your place in Christ is a place of ELEVATION, seated together with Christ who is seated far above principality, and power, and might, and dominion, and every name that is named. (Ephesians 1:21)

Ask the Holy Spirit to reveal to you the position you have in Christ. You are more than a conqueror who ALWAYS triumphs in Christ. (Romans 8:37, 2 Corinthians 2:14)

Remember, Paul wrote many of these words from prison. Which tells me that victory and triumph are not about your physical condition but your spiritual position. Your position in Christ!! Praise God!!

Here is what God's word says in Isaiah 60:1-2 *"Arise, shine; for thy light is come, and the glory of the Lord is risen upon thee. For, behold, the darkness shall cover the earth, and thick darkness the people: but the Lord shall arise upon thee, and his glory shall be seen upon thee."*

Elevate and Illuminate for the glory of the Lord is risen (elevated) upon you. Notice that you can be surrounded by darkness but still have glory and light on you.

Don't let what's around you affect what is in and on you. It's time to ELEVATE! Rise up and be the church, people, and families that God has called, ordained, and anointed us to be in Jesus Name!! ELEVATE!

25-DAY
LIFE LESSONS

RECHARGE!

Day 1 - DON'T BE DECEIVED

Deception. Not a word we use a lot but one that has been on my mind for a few days. Let's look at what deception is and the different aspects of being deceived.

Paul wrote to the church at Corinth in 2 Corinthians 11:3 and said he was concerned that they might be deceived just as the serpent deceived Eve.

To deceive means to cause a person to believe something that is not true with the intent of gaining a personal advantage. Why does the enemy want to deceive us? To gain an advantage over us. He wants to convince us to believe a lie. He knows that the truth will set us free so he seeks to distort the truth and cause us to believe a twisted truth.

The heart of deception is not believing an outright lie but believing a twisted truth. Look at how the serpent deceived Eve. He took God's word, twisted the truth, Eve believed a twisted truth and was deceived.

Satan even tried to twist and distort God's word when tempting Jesus in the wilderness. Just think: Satan tried to distort the word to 'THE WORD', Jesus.

If he will try to deceive Jesus into believing a lie then I can promise you he will try to trick us into believing a lie.

The heart of deception is the twisting of truth and the belief of a partial truth, especially when it comes to God's word.

Another element of deception is using God's word to justify our beliefs instead of our beliefs being justified by God's word. God's Word is the final authority for our lives. If we constantly search and study His word to back up our own ideas then we enter a state of deception. Why? Because we no longer seek Him and His Word for what it is but for what we want it to be and therefore limiting our perception to receive truth.

Here's one remedy to help avoid deception in our lives. James 1:22 says to "*Be doers of the word and not hearers only, deceiving your own selves.*"

The number one way to avoid being deceived in our lives is to obey the Word when we hear. Hearing God's word over and over but never obeying, allows the enemy of our souls to come in and convince us that what we are hearing is for everyone else except us.

Being "doers" of the word is the equivalent of obeying God's Word. If Eve would have been a doer of the Word (obeyed), then she would not have been deceived.

Study the Word. Hear the Word. Believe the Word. Receive the Word. Obey the Word. May the Lord give us all the Spirit of discernment to do what He has called us to do.

Be blessed in the mighty Name of Jesus

Day 2 - WHAT'S LOVE GOT TO DO WITH IT? - I

In the words of the popular song, "What's love got to do with it?" The answer: Everything!

Love is at the very center of the Gospel. The message of the gospel is not so much redemption, salvation, or regeneration as much as it is love. These may be extremely important in our relationship with God but are by-products of love. John 3:16 does not say For God so wanted to redeem the world that He gave, or for God so wanted to save the world that He gave. John 3:16 says *"For God so LOVED the world that He gave His only begotten son."*

Yes, the Son of man came to seek and save that which was lost (Luke 19:10) but He did so because He loves. 1 John 4:8 takes it a step further and says the *"God is love."*

Just a couple thoughts: If the message of the gospel is love and if God is love, then what should be the focus of our walk with Christ? Yep, you guessed it, LOVE.

This is easier said than done sometimes. I know they say let things roll of you like water off a duck's back but face it, we aren't ducks. We have feelings, emotions, and we have our flesh to deal with in many instances.

Still yet, we are encouraged continually in scripture to "walk in love." (Ephesians 5:2) 1 John 2:10 says the prerequisite for remaining in the light of God is walking in love.

All of our actions, words, and deeds should be motivated out of:

1 - love for our Lord, 2 - love for our fellow brothers and sisters in the Lord, and 3 - love for mankind to see them redeemed to the Lord.

Love is a fruit of the Spirit which means it cannot be imitated, manufactured, or conceived through the flesh. The ability to love like Christ loves us cannot be done or accomplished outside of the working of the Holy Spirit in our lives. It requires a renewing of our mind, a crucifying of our flesh, and a building up of our spirit-man.

I will end this devotion with this thought to provide a little bit of balance. Walking in love does not require you to be a doormat or to let anything go. The Bible also teaches us that the ones God loves He also disciplines. Sometimes walking in love requires discipline but even then, the discipline should be done in the spirit of love.

Day 3 –
WHAT'S LOVE GOT TO DO WITH IT? - II

What is the one sign Jesus said would show that we are His disciples? John 13:35 does not say, by this shall all men know that you are my disciples, if you are good singers and preachers or if you have good church programs.

The distinguishing mark of a believer is that we love one another.

Many times, we focus on what we do: the singing, preaching, and programs instead of who we are: love.

Don't get me wrong, all these things are good but can be done without love. Without love, what we do can easily become lifeless and void of effectiveness.

Galatians 5:6 even tells us that even our walk of faith is determined by our ability to walk in love: Faith works through love. We've heard many teachings on Faith and how our lives need to be full of faith. While this is true, Paul also told us in 1 Corinthians 13:13 that *"Faith, Hope, and Love abide, the greatest of the three is Love."*

We see, then, that Love is greater than faith. Love is greater than gifts. 1 Corinthians 13 is sandwiched in between chapters 12 and 14 which deal with the operation of the gifts of the Spirit within the Body of Christ. Gifts without Love will always end up being used for selfish gain and personal edification instead of the edifying of the Body. Operating in the gifts should always be tempered and balanced out by walking in love.

There are nine gifts of the Spirit in 1 Corinthians 12 and nine fruits of the Spirit listed in Galatians 5. Paul, the apostle, also wrote in chapter 13 of 1 Corinthians *"And though I have the gift of prophecy, and understand all mysteries, and all knowledge; and though I have all faith, so that I could move mountains, and have not charity, I am nothing. And though I bestow all my goods to feed the poor, and though I give my body to be burned, and have not charity, it profiteth me nothing."*

Day 4 –
WHATS LOVE GOT TO DO WITH IT? - III

"But if ye bite and devour one another, take heed that ye be not consumed one of another." Galatians 5:15

I think it is interesting and worth noting the position of this scripture in chapter 5 of Galatians. Verse 14 says *"For the whole law is fulfilled in one word: "You shall love your neighbor as yourself."* Then verse 16 is *"But I say, walk by the Spirit, and you will not gratify the desires of the flesh."*

Biting and devouring one another is right in between loving your neighbor and walking in the Spirit. Paul then goes on to list the desires of the flesh. This list of fleshly desires includes: enmity, strife, jealousy, fits of anger, rivalries, dissensions, divisions, and envy.

That's a pretty serious list, especially given the fact that these acts are listed along with adultery and sorcery. To go one step further with this point, 1 Corinthians 3:3 reads like this, *"for you are still of the flesh. For while there is jealousy and strife among you, are you not of the flesh and behaving only in a human way?"*

These few passages of scripture clearly show us one very important aspect of walking in

70

love. The number one enemy of believers walking in love is not the devil or demons. It is our flesh. Granted, the enemy may throw stumbling blocks and situations our way to trip us up but the ultimate decision is ours. We have to choose to walk in love just as we have to choose to walk by faith.

I have to be honest and transparent here. I've been tested on many occasions on my love walk since the first devotional on walking in love was posted. I would love to tell you that I passed with flying colors, but I haven't. I didn't fail either. I would give myself somewhere around a B-minus. I repeat, 'walking in love is easier said than done!' It requires the crucifying of our flesh which is one of the biggest obstacles every believer faces.

Let us all heed the very serious warning in Galatians 5:15 and take note that not walking in love starts a vicious cycle which will cause believers to self-destruct and implode from the inside out by devouring one another. The enemy does not need to try and devour us when we are devouring one another. Satan is the accuser of the brethren and many times uses other believers to do the accusing.

Once again, this is not an anything goes doctrine to walk in love. But it is a call, that even though we may have to discipline or correct other believers, we should still do it in the spirit of love.

These passages of scripture deal with a constant and continual dismantling of other believers that result in the tearing apart of the Body of Christ. Darkness cannot exist in and of itself. Darkness is the absence of light. Hate cannot exist in and of itself. Hate is the absence of love. The absence of love is an absence of God because God is love. Any area of our life void of love is also void of God. Let's all be encouraged to let the love of God permeate our very being. Pray like this, "Lord, let me see people the way you see people. Let me love people the way you love people." I trust this installment on walking in love has helped and challenged you as much as I've been challenged.

God bless you in Jesus' Name!

Day 5 - HELP IS ON THE WAY

"Wherefore, holy brethren, partakers of the heavenly calling, consider the Apostle and High Priest of our profession, Christ Jesus." Hebrews 3:1

This verse tells us that Jesus is the Apostle and High Priest of our profession or our Confession. Many scholars believe that Apostle is a reference to Moses, who ministered For God, and High Priest is a reference to Aaron who ministered to God. Moses would bring God's Word to the people and Aaron would take the people's request (primarily sacrifices for sin offerings) to God.

The Bible says that there is one Mediator between God and Man and that is Jesus. So Jesus, as intercessor, takes our requests to the Father, and then based upon those requests brings the answer back to us through revelation of the Holy Spirit.

Notice what He is the Apostle and High Priest over: OUR CONFESSION. Confession means to acknowledge the covenant. It partially comes from the Greek word LOGOS which is the written Word. The word LOGOS comes from the Greek word LEGO.

Sound familiar? Lego's are building block toys

for kids. The significance is that our Confession is the building blocks for our life.

Not only that, but Jesus, Himself is watching over that confession. Here's one of the ways He makes the confession come to pass.

Hebrews 1:14 talks of how the angels are ministering spirits sent forth to minister for the Heirs of Salvation. That's all the born again, blood-washed believers.

Psalm 119:89 says that God's word is forever settled in Heaven. The word settled means Established. So God's word is established. It's set, unchangeable, and unalterable. You cannot change God's word.

Psalm 103:20 says that the angels do HIS commandments hearken to the VOICE of HIS word. Hearken means to hear and obey. Look closely, it does not necessarily say that the angels hearken to His voice, even though they do. It says they hear and obey the voice of His WORD. By our Confession, we give VOICE to His word. In other words, when we begin to acknowledge the covenant (confess) and come into agreement with the word that is forever settled in Heaven, that Jesus is watching over that confession but the angels also are hearing what we say.

Note: we should NEVER pray to angels or seek their guidance. We are ALWAYS to seek the guidance of the Holy Spirit. However, when we begin to speak the Word of God over ourselves and our situations, Jesus can then release those ministering spirits to come and minister for the Heirs of salvation.

So don't give up. Help is on the way! It may or may not come immediately but don't give up. Daniel prayed for 21 days before the answer came. In Daniel 10:12-13, the angel told Daniel *"I heard you the first time you prayed, but the prince of Persia withstood me."* The angel was released the first time Daniel prayed and the answer was released but there was some spiritual warfare going on that held up the answer.

We sometimes want to put a magic formula on the 21 days. However, I believe that Daniel would have petitioned God until the answer came. Sometimes we have to pray UNTIL. Keep praying until the answer comes, until the healing comes, until the breakthrough manifests in our lives. In verse 12 of Daniel 10 the angel told Daniel *"I have come because of your WORDS."*

Be encouraged and don't stop confessing God's Word. There may be some warfare right now, but your answer has already been released.

DON'T GIVE UP!!!!! HELP IS ON THE WAY!!!!!!

Day 6 - HE'S ABLE

Here's a question for you: Why do people pray for healing, strength, salvation, or deliverance?

The answer: because they believe that God is able.

The fact is, you don't go to a bank to borrow money unless you truly believe the bank has the money to give. You would not let a doctor perform surgery on you unless you believed he had the ability to do the surgery. So it is with God.

The reason you ask is 1) Because He told us to ask, and 2) Because He is able to grant the petitions we ask of Him.

The word able means to have power or be capable. There are accounts throughout all the Bible of the power and capability of God. He alone is the Ever Present, All-Powerful, All-Knowing God.

One such instance is in Daniel 3. Shadrach, Meshach, and Abednego refused to worship the golden image set up by Nebuchadnezzar and were about to be thrown into the fiery furnace. Verses 17 and 18 reveal an interesting aspect about faith. They declare to the king that God is ABLE to deliver them from the furnace and from the king's hand. However, in verse 18 they said this, *"But if not, be it known unto thee, O King, that we will not serve thy gods, nor worship the golden image."*

WHAT A STATEMENT!! In essence, they were saying, "We know God is able, but if He doesn't deliver us, we still will not serve your gods." Some would say that is not a great confession of faith, but I believe it uncovers a truth at the heart of faith.

Faith is not telling God when, where, how, and what He needs to do but is just knowing He is God. Believe and trust in God and leave the results up to Him.

God did deliver them but not in the way most would want. They still had to go into the fire to be delivered. Just because God did not show up when and where you wanted Him to does not mean that He's not going to show up at all. Many times we want the power without the process.

You have to understand that many times, it is the process that produces the power. There's purpose to your process. The process is making you stronger, better, purer, more anointed, and wiser. Don't place your faith in when he will answer. Put your faith in the fact that He will answer and take you through the fire if that is what is required. Know beyond the shadow of a doubt that He is able to keep you from falling during the process.

He is able to do exceeding abundantly for you. For he that comes to God must believe that He is and that He is a rewarder of those who diligently seek Him. (Hebrews 11:6)

Keep the faith and be blessed

in Jesus' Name!!!

Day 7 - HIS GRACE IS SUFFICIENT

It's been a busy week in the Roberts' house. Then again, when is it not a busy week? At any rate, here's a little food for thought. We use the scripture that God's grace is sufficient. Sometimes it's used more often than other times depending on where we are or what we are facing in life.

It sounds great and very spiritual at face value but what does it really mean? Honestly, how many times do we say things that are spiritual but still don't get a full grasp on what we are saying? What does sufficient mean?

Here's how Webster's dictionary defines it: Enough to meet the needs of a situation or to suffice. Suffice means to meet a need, be capable, and comes from a Latin root which means to provide.

There's not a lot of glitz and glamour to the definition but when placed in the context of the scripture and with the word "Grace," it makes more sense.

2 Corinthians 12 gives the account of Paul seeking the Lord to remove the thorn in his flesh (a messenger of Satan). He prayed three times and nothing happened. Finally, the

Lord's response is *"My grace is sufficient."* His grace is capable to meet the need and provide.

Relying on God's grace removes us and our works from the equation. Depending on His grace is harder than doing things ourselves.

We feel like we have to work, toil, and struggle for everything but Grace is the opposite of that. Grace comes when we don't deserve it, when we don't work for it, and many times when we don't expect it. Grace brings us to a position of trusting and believing God for Who is in our lives.

You see, Paul wanted deliverance, but God gave him grace. In this instance God was saying, "you don't need delivered. You just need My grace." Why? Because His grace is sufficient.

The heart of Grace is God's good will, loving kindness and favor.

We always feel like we need something. More money, a better car, a better job, a new house, and the list goes on and on. BUT, the fact is, if we have God's favor, the list will take care of itself and becomes much less important.

God's grace not only saves you, but sustains you. The principle is that all your needs are met because of and through the grace (good will and favor) of God.

Whatever you are facing today, know that His grace will sustain, uphold, and provide for whatever you need. Depend on Him. Rely totally on Him. He will not let you fail or fall. His Grace is sufficient.

God bless your day in Jesus' Name!

Day 8 - THE CURE FOR CARE

Proverbs 3:5 says *"Trust in the Lord with all your heart and lean not to your own understanding."*

Trust is to the Old Testament what Faith is to the New Testament. Faith is only mentioned twice in the entire Old Testament writings, but trust is mentioned 107 different times. The definitions are very similar though.

Trust means to be bold, confident, or to be careless.

I like to read this as CARE-LESS, which means the absence of care. This doesn't mean to have an I don't care about anything attitude. It is, however, to be free from worry, anxiety and concern.

Worry is our inability to trust in the ability of our God. 1 Peter 5:7 tells us to cast all of our care upon Him, for He cares for us. So Proverbs 3:5 is encouraging us to be "Care-less" in the Lord but also goes on to say what the opposite of being care-less means: Lean not to your own understanding.

Lean means to support one's self or rely upon. In other words, don't try to support or rely upon yourself because when you do, you place yourself in a position where your understand-

83

ing takes over. This is where you know better than God and have things figured out according to "your" plan. When this happens, you will always find yourself in a position of "standing under" the promises of God for your life.

Relying upon one's self tells God that His help is not needed. It also brings the care that He has promised to carry upon you, and therefore the anxiety and worry are now your responsibility as well.

TRUST IS THE CURE FOR CARE.

Isaiah 26:3 gives us a promise of perfect peace when we keep our mind (understanding) fixed on the Lord. The only reason you can keep your mind on Him is because you trust Him. The mind will automatically focus on what it has been trained to trust. You trust Him because you know Him.

Think about all the times He brought you out, made a way when there was no way, or fulfilled a promise that looked seemingly impossible to accomplish. Purposely remind yourself of the goodness of the Lord. Know that His grace is sufficient for any problem or situation you may be facing.

He has not saved you to forsake you. He did not call you to abandon you. He didn't redeem you to reject you.

Psalm 62:8 *"Trust in Him at all times; ye people, pour out your heart before Him: God is a refuge for us."*

Give Him the care. Give Him the worry. Give Him the anxiety and concern. Pour out your heart to Him in prayer, trust that He will direct your path, and take refuge that He IS a promise-keeping God.

Day 9 - WHAT REALLY MATTERS?

I've been thinking this evening about what really matters in life. The answer to this question will change considerably depending on who is asked.

Answers will range from: family, kids, spouse, job, God, church, ministry, and the possibilities are endless. Then, once we get a top five list we try to prioritize from 1-5 in order of importance. Most Christian teaching has taught us to do this and further gives us the order 1-God, 2-Family, 3-Church, 4-Job and so on.

The concept is good but can easily lead to a compartmentalized life where each one gets its own amount of time. The question then becomes if God is number one then how much time does He get? How much time does our family get? If you have to work overtime on your job and put 55 hours in for one week, but only pray or read your Bible for a total of 20 hours, then the priority list is shot.

That doesn't mention feeling like the family has now been neglected. And what happens when the demands of ministry enter the equation and you find yourself totally engaged in religious activity and put it under category number one and think it is God.

Just a note - It's easy to be doing the work of the Lord and forget about the Lord of the work. (Bear with me as I share). Maybe God doesn't really want to be a number on a priority list. Maybe families don't want to consistently feel second place to church or jobs. MAYBE the priority list is well intentioned but ultimately keeps people in a form of religion and keeps them bound by the very list they've created. Just maybe God doesn't want to be number one on a list but at the center of everything you do in life.

Priority lists are very goal-oriented but not always Glory-oriented. Having goals is great and biblical. But sometimes we can be so motivated by accomplishing goals that we forget God. I'm not trying to ruffle feathers but am wanting to make you evaluate. You see the answer to 'What really Matters' determines what is at the center of what you do.

The Apostle Paul wrote *"that I may know Him."* He considered all his accomplishments as dung (poo, LOL) in comparison to knowing Jesus. Paul understood that at the end of the day, the only thing that really matters is knowing Jesus.

Most of us measure success based upon worldly standards, visible criteria, and did we get what we wanted. How much money we make.

How nice of a house or car we have. How big our churches are, or how many have been healed or saved. There's nothing wrong with any of these things, but Paul measured success by something no one can see, "Do we know Jesus?" Not do we go to church, sing in the choir, work in the children's or youth ministry.

Do we really know Jesus? Is He at the center of everything we do? Keep this in mind - success is not determined by man and his view of you but if you hear Jesus say, "Well done, good and faithful servant."

Be blessed.

Day 10 - GETTING OUT OF THE WILDERNESS

I was preaching recently, and the Lord gave me a saying that I can't get out of my head. I had a good theologically sound, three-point sermon together and didn't use any notes. The Lord gave me one word, FREEDOM, and the scripture in Galatians 5:1 *"Stand fast therefore in the liberty wherein Christ has made you free and be not entangled again with the yoke of bondage."*

I ended up talking about the children of Israel, how God miraculously delivered them out of Egypt (bondage), and then led them by His Glory through the wilderness. The wilderness is the process the Lord took them through. He told them why they were in the wilderness in Deuteronomy 8. It was to humble them and prove them so He could do them good in their latter end. God is not interested in our short term satisfaction near as much as He is interested in His long term fulfillment.

The wilderness may not be good right now, but the latter end will be good. God uses the wilderness as the process to work things out of us. If we don't get it out of us on this level (the process) it will kill us in the next (the promise).

Everybody has to go through a wilderness experience at some point in their life. So, here's the quote from that sermon: "Leading you through the wilderness is up to God. How long you stay in the wilderness is up to us." We can extend our wilderness by what we do and how we act while we're there. Our response determines our reward.

The problem I see with the Israelites is every time an issue or problem arose, they wanted to go back to Egypt (bondage). It's easy for us to judge them and say, "I can't believe they would want to go back to slavery," but many of us do the same thing. If we're really honest, we've all wanted to throw in the towel and quit. Thank God for His Grace and Mercy that would not let us! You also have to keep in mind that they were being led by the Glory of the Lord the entire time.

Here's a news flash: Sometimes being led by the Spirit and following the Glory will take you into the wilderness. Even Jesus went through a wilderness experience. Luke 4 tells us that Jesus was full of the Holy Spirit and was led by the Spirit to the wilderness to be tempted.

Being full of the Holy Spirit does not exempt us from the wilderness. Rather, it will lead us there to fortify the anointing God has placed on the inside of us. So be encouraged today if you feel like you are in a wilderness experience.

God has not placed you there to punish you but to prove you. He's just taking you through the process to get you to the promotion. Remember, He will lead you to and through it, but how long you stay there is up to you.

I believe David's prayer in Psalm 51 will get us out a little quicker. *"Create in me a clean heart and renew a right spirit within me."*

Have a blessed day
in the Mighty Name of Jesus!

Day 11 - TAKE THE MASK OFF!

I'm not trying to sermonize or teach a subject as much as I'm wanting to just share from my heart and make us all think a little today.

I've thought a lot about the "masks" we all wear when we come to church services, church events, and hang around other church folk. In too many Christian circles, people put on a facade and try to be something they are not in order to fit in with the status quo of the culture they are in. It's the whole "you gotta look like me, act like me, talk like me, sing like me, preach like me, teach like me" to meet the bar.

When this is the dominant culture, people become more like trading baseball cards than living, breathing souls. The question then becomes not about who you are, but what have you done? Who do you know? Or what can you do for me? This mentality only keeps people in bondage.

Let's face the facts. People are human and make mistakes, say things they shouldn't, and do things they shouldn't. Yes, we should strive for perfection. But the image of perfection is not looking at other human beings but looking at the Word of God and Jesus Christ.

2 Corinthians 10:12 says we are not wise when we measure and compare ourselves with ourselves. Whenever we try to mimic the image of another person, we limit the ability of our creator to form us into HIS image. We have to have a culture of acceptance that leads and brings people to true freedom in Christ.

I believe one of the number one tactics the enemy uses to keep others from getting saved and staying saved as Christians.

Most people like to use the word "hypocrite" when describing Christians. No one intentionally wants or tries to be a hypocrite. Most believers are almost forced into the category of hypocrite because they are trying to wear the mask and be something they are not. Afraid to make mistakes. Scared that someone may find out that they actually have a problem or struggle with sin.

Jesus says in Matthew 11:28, *"Come unto me all ye who labor and are heavy laden and I will give you rest."*

I want to encourage you. Be who you are. Just be real and be what GOD has created you to be. This is not a license to be rude, unkind, hateful, or to habitually practice sin. But this is a wakeup call to see who we really are now AND to see who the Lord really wants us to be.

Jesus will take you from where you are and lead you to where you need to be.

Take the mask off! Have a blessed day.

Day 12 - FOCUS, DON'T FAINT

I'm really preaching to the choir on this one today. Most of the time, I have to chew on it before I can give it out. This is one of those instances. I pray that you are encouraged and uplifted as you read. Have a blessed day.

Hebrews 12:2-3 says, "Looking unto Jesus the author and finisher of our faith; who for the joy that was set before him endured the cross, despising the shame, and is set down at the right hand of the throne of God. For consider him that endured such contradiction of sinners against himself, lest ye be wearied and faint in your minds."

What has captured your attention? What things, events, situations, or people always seem to be at the center of your life?

Whatever has your attention will determine your direction. Yet, here is an admonition in scripture for us to look unto Jesus. The word "looking" has the meaning of turning from something in order to look to something else. Many times in life, you will have to look away from those things that constantly demand your attention and make a conscious, determined decision to look unto Jesus.

The reason we can to look to Him is because He is the author and finisher of our faith. What HE starts, He finishes. What HE promises, He will perform. Look at your life as a book and Jesus as the author. The pages of your life are already written in the history book of eternity. Your destiny has already been declared. Isaiah 46:10 says that God declares the end from the beginning and from ancient times the things that are not yet done. He knew and had purposed your ending before you ever started. Psalm 138:8 further encourages us that *"The Lord will perfect (complete, finish, take care of) that which concerneth me."*

The Lord is already taking care of the things you are concerned about. Praise God! What a promise! Focusing on Jesus will bring a confidence that He is able to complete what He started.

Verse 3 of Hebrews 12 gives us the key, *"Consider Him…lest ye be wearied and faint in your minds."* Consider means an intense repetition. So, what are we to intensely repeat in our minds? *"For consider Him who endured such hostility by sinners against Himself."* In other words, Concentrate on the Cross. This is an admonishment that if Jesus endured the scourging, beating, shame, pain, whipping and punishment of the cross, then we can perse-vere and be victorious as well.

Greater is He that is in You than he that is in the world. Focusing on His finished work on the cross and His Resurrection will help keep life's difficulties in perspective and will prevent you from fainting in your mind.

Don't give up! Focus, don't Faint.

Day 13 - LET'S GO MOUNTAIN CLIMBING

I have been thinking about Mountains and Valleys. One represents victories. The other represents struggles. One represents accomplishment. The other represents failure. It's not hard to figure out which represents which.

Everyone loves mountain experiences. The biggest issue with mountain experiences is you have to walk through the valley before you can get to the mountain experience.

I truly believe that those who appear to be standing on the highest mountain have also had to walk through the lowest valleys to get there. The height of your mountain is directly proportional to the depth of your valley. Extremely high mountains also make for extremely low valleys.

No one wants to walk through the valley. Even David wrote inPsalm 23:4, *"Even though I walk through the valley of the shadow of death, I fear no evil, for You are with me."*

Always keep in mind, you were never intended to stay in the valley. Don't stop in the valley. Walk THROUGH it! Dreams die in the valley and Discouragement lives in the valley. Don't stop in the valley. Go through it.

Notice it is called the valley of the shadow of

death. Question: What causes the shadow? Answer: The mountain you are about to climb. The same thing that is the sign of your victory is also the same thing that is causing your shadow now.

Your greatest victories are a result of your greatest battles. Your greatest successes usually rest on the back of your biggest struggles.

Here's the key to success in the valley: Don't be fearful because God is with you. People may leave you in the valley, but Jesus will not. He promised to never leave you or forsake you. Rest in His Presence. Walk in His Power. Live in His Promises. The valley is just part of the path to get you to the top of the mountain.

Be encouraged if you're in the valley and know it is not your final destination. You are just on your way to the top of the mountain. Here's a little strength for your journey:

Psalm 121:1-8: *"I will lift up my eyes to the hills - From whence comes my help? My help comes from the LORD, Who made heaven and earth. He will not allow your foot to be moved; He who keeps you will not slumber. Behold, He who keeps Israel shall neither slumber nor sleep. The LORD is your keeper; the LORD is your shade at your right hand. The sun shall not strike you by day, nor the moon by night.*

The LORD shall preserve you from all evil; He shall preserve your soul. The LORD shall preserve your going out and your coming in, from this time forth, and even forevermore."

Day 14 - BE ENCOURAGED

"And David was greatly distressed; for the people spake of stoning him, because the soul of all the people was grieved, every man for his sons and for his daughters: but David encouraged himself in the LORD his God." 1 Samuel 30:6

David was stressed out. Yes, the mighty king. The man after God's own heart was stressed. Sound familiar? I know most of the people reading this never get stressed out, so this is for the rest of us. LOL. Notice the source of David's stress, *"for the people spake."* David was in a position to where he could not look to anyone else for encouragement. So what did he do? He encouraged himself. Well, Praise God!

The key, though, is that he encouraged himself IN the Lord. The only real source of encouragement comes from the Lord. Encourage means to inspire with courage, spirit, or hope. Courage is mental or moral strength to venture, persevere and withstand danger, fear, or difficulty. Courage and strength always go hand in hand.

Joshua 1:9 says *"Have not I commanded thee? Be strong and of a good courage; be not afraid, neither be thou dismayed: for the LORD thy God is with thee whithersoever thou goest."* The reason you can take courage and be strong is because God is with you wherever you go. The King of Kings and Lord of Lords is working for you, not against you. And if God be for you, who can be against you? That is reason enough to rejoice and be encouraged. To help out a little more, here are three things that will help you to encourage yourself:

1 - REMEMBER PAST VICTORIES. Let's go back to David when he was younger and about to face Goliath. Here's a young boy getting ready to fight a giant that an entire army was afraid to confront. What gave David the courage to fight Goliath? He remembered his past victories. 1 Samuel 17:37 - *"David said moreover, The LORD that delivered me out of the paw of the lion, and out of the paw of the bear, he will deliver me out of the hand of this Philistine."* Essentially he was saying, "If God delivered me out of that, He will deliver me out of this!'"

2 - GET IN GOD'S WORD. Psalm 119:114 – *"You are my hiding place and my shield; I hope in Your word."* There is hope in the Word of God. Find a promise in the scripture. Claim it. Believe it. Declare it. Let it bring hope to you that God's word never fails.

3 – PRAY. Ephesians 3:16 *"That He would grant you, according to the riches of His glory, to be strengthened with might through His Spirit in the inner man."* This passage of scripture is included in a prayer that Paul was praying for the believers in Ephesus. It clearly shows that strength comes from the inner man (your spirit) through prayer. Prayer will build up your spirit and cause you to have faith in the midst of impossible situations. Be Encouraged today. Rest in the fact that God is God. And that He is in control.

God bless your day in Jesus' mighty name.

Day 15 - SEASONS

We've heard a lot said about seasons in church. Generally, it is a Pastor or preacher sharing from their heart what they believe is the next season for them or for the ministry. This is good and I believe many times it is a word from the Lord. However, you have to have discernment from the Holy Spirit as to how or if it may apply to you and your life.

I've thought much about the changing of seasons in regard to why and how they change. There are several factors that involve the changing of seasons in the natural. And I believe there is generally a spiritual truth connected to the natural. Seasons in the natural begin changing in the atmosphere before we see them materialize. The Earth's rotation and distance from the Sun begins to shift before the leaves start falling or the temperature begins to rise or fall. Spiritual truth: You will have a sense that your season is about to change in your spirit before you ever see anything changing in your sight. Be sensitive to where the Holy Spirit is leading and what you are sensing. Get some trusted prayer partners, men and or women of God who will pray with you.

The season of harvest begins in the spring with

the planting of seeds. Then those seeds are cultivated until harvest time. You can take the right seed, plant it in the right soil, but if you do it in the wrong season, it will not grow. For instance, during the winter, plants lie dormant and some animals go into hibernation. Sometimes it's ok to lie dormant for a season. Just don't get used to it. I believe there are some reading this who are about to come out of spiritual hibernation and others may be about to do some hibernation. And the great thing about it is: both are right. You simply have to know what the Holy Spirit is wanting you to do for your current season.

Seasons come and seasons go. The main point I want to make is, do the right thing in the right season.

Ecclesiastes 3: 1-8 says it like this:
"To everything there is a season,
A time for every purpose under heaven:
A time to be born, And a time to die; A time to
plant, And a time to pluck what is planted;
A time to kill, And a time to heal;
A time to break down, And a time to build up;
A time to weep, And a time to laugh;
A time to mourn, And a time to dance;
A time to cast away stones, And a time to
gather stones; A time to embrace,
And a time to refrain from embracing;
A time to gain, And a time to lose;

A time to keep, And a time to throw away;
A time to tear, and a time to sew;
A time to keep silence, and a time to speak;
A time to love, and a time to hate;
A time of war, and a time of peace."

You may be in war right now. Don't worry. It's only a season. Peace will come. You may be mourning right now. Don't worry. It's only a season. Dancing will come. You may be weeping right now. Don't worry. It's only a season. Laughter will return. Let the Lord be your guide. He will lead you and walk with you whatever your season may be.

Day 16 - PRAYER

Prayer is often talked about but rarely practiced. Prayer is one of the simplest, most important practices a believer has. The gifts are activated through prayer. Revelation is birthed through prayer. Direction is given through prayer. Cleansing of the soul from sin is found in prayer.

One of the keys is having faith when you pray. Our faith is connected to our endurance. Hebrews 10:36 says that we have need of patience. Patience there actually means endurance. Prayer without faith is like a vehicle without gas. We can sit in a car all we want to, but if there's no gas in the tank, the vehicle isn't going anywhere. It takes a measure of faith to ask but even more faith to endure until you see the answer come.

Matthew 7:7 is a very misquoted scripture. (even by me. LOL) Most people quote it "Ask and you shall receive." However, it actually says, *"Ask and it shall be given."*

God gives the answer as soon as you ask, but many times it takes endurance and faith to keep believing until you receive what it is you have been asking for. That is why this scripture literally means to Ask and keep on Asking.

Daniel 10 tells of how Daniel was fasting and praying for an answer. The angel Gabriel finally shows up with the answer 21 days later and tells Daniel, "I was sent with the message the first day you prayed but was withstood by the Prince of Persia." A heavenly prince was fighting the answer to his prayer.

Ephesians 6 tells us we wrestle against principalities. ("PRINCE"-ipalities). You have to understand that Satan will fight your answer from coming. He knows that if he can delay the answer long enough then you just may give up on asking.

Don't be discouraged by a delayed answer. I believe that Daniel's ENDURANCE (faith) to keep on praying is what fueled the heavenly battle and eventually brought the answer.

You may be on "day 20" and want to give up. BUT you have a "day 21" moment coming. Don't give up on God. Keep the faith. Keep on Believing. Keep fueling the vehicle of prayer with your faith. Pray! Pray! Pray! Your help is coming and you will reap if you faint not.

Day 17 - SEASONS OF SEPARATION

Genesis 32:24: *"Then Jacob was left alone, and a man wrestled with him until daybreak."*

Mark 4:34: *"But without a parable spake he not unto them: and when they were alone, he expounded all things to his disciples."*

Nobody really wants or likes to be alone. Some people even have an innate fear of being alone. Some go from one bad relationship to another for fear of being alone or because of undealt abandonment issues. Others are always in a crowd or with friends for a fear of being alone.

Alone means separation and isolation. God Himself said in Genesis 2:18 that it is not good for man to be alone. However, I believe God takes us through seasons of isolation and separation. These seasons of being "alone" produce results in us that would not be produced otherwise.

Jacob had a life changing, destiny altering, undeniable experience with the Lord after he was "left alone." Jesus explained things to His disciples when they were alone so that the crowd could not hear. Separation will lead us to seek Him and Him alone. Seasons of isolation will generally bring revelation.

John wrote the book of Revelation while isolated on the isle of Patmos. Isolation, separation, and being alone allows us to focus more clearly on Jesus and hearing HIS voice. Daniel saw a great vision when he was alone. (Daniel 10:8). Being alone is mainly about perspective. If you look at it as though you are being punished or disciplined, then you will dread it. If you perceive that you are all by yourself, then you will fear it. However, if you see being alone as a temporary season to hear God, experience His presence, and know His voice like never before, then you will embrace this time.

The fact is, you're never really alone anyhow. Jesus said in Matthew 28:20 that He is with us always. You may feel as though you are separated from people, but I can promise you that you are never separated from Jesus.

Be encouraged, your season of separation is merely a time for the Lord to speak to you and give you fresh insight, strength, and revelation. Stay faithful to Him. You will make it through.

Day 18 - PROMISES

Genesis 22 tells of the account where God asked Abraham to sacrifice his promise on the altar. Not just any promise but THE promise; Abraham's only son.

There will be times in our lives when God will ask us to do things that will not make logical sense and require us to walk by faith. Abraham did not doubt or ask questions. He just obeyed.

How was he able to obey such a hard request? Hebrews 11:17-19 gives us the answer, *"By faith Abraham, when he was tried, offered up Isaac: and he that had received the promises offered up his only begotten son, Of whom it was said, That in Isaac shall thy seed be called: Accounting that God was able to raise him up,"*

Abraham believed that if God gave the promise to start with, that He could also resurrect that same promise. Abraham's confession of faith in Genesis 22:5 stated,*"I and the boy go to wor- ship and WE will be back!"*

Abraham already knew he and Isaac would re- turn. He didn't know HOW it was going to work but he knew it WAS going to work out. May your faith be strengthened today as you believe that even the seemingly dead promises in your life will be resurrected!

Day 19 - HE'S A FAITHFUL FATHER

James 1:17 - *"Every good gift and every perfect gift is from above, and cometh down from the Father of lights, with whom is no variableness, neither shadow of turning."*

James 1:5 says God is Light and in Him is no darkness.

1 John 4 tells us that God is Love. Very clearly the Bible reveals to us the nature of God; Light and Love. If God is light and love then we must be able to conclude that Satan is darkness and hate. This shows us that God operates in the realm of light and love, and Satan can only operate in the realm of darkness and hate.

The God who is light and love is therefore the Father, or originator, of every good gift. John 10:10 says, *"the thief comes to steal, kill, and destroy but I (Jesus, the God of light and love) have come that you might have life and that you may have it more abundantly."*

Our great God is also the Father of every perfect gift. The word *perfect* means wanting nothing necessary to completeness. What God gives will always complete you and your life, and never leave you feeling empty. The fake promises of the adversary will always leave you wanting for more.

113

Jesus, in John chapter 4, encountered a woman from Samaria. This woman was there to draw out water for her and her family when Jesus made a bold statement, "I will give you water so you never thirst again."

Everything Satan and the world offers will always leave us thirsting for more. One drink from the well of salvation can bring a completeness to your life that you have never known.

Day 20 - VARIABLENESS

James 1:17 says there is no variableness with God nor shadow of turning. Variableness is a good King James Version word.

Seriously, when is the last time, if ever, you used the word variableness in a sentence? Just a thought. Even when considering the outdated nature of the word, the meaning brings out great truth about our faithful Father. Variableness means fickle. That's right, this literally means God is not fickle.

Now everyone has probably use some variation of the word fickle to describe someone. Inconsistent, 'some-timey', fake, you never know about them, one day they're your friend and the next day they're not, are all words and phrases that describe fickle. Essentially, all these words can be summed up by saying a person is unfaithful in their friendship.

But God is not fickle or unfaithful. God is always faithful. 2 Timothy 2:13 says if we are faithless, He still remains faithful.

Praise God that He has remained faithful in your life even when you were not. He remained consistent even if you did not.

Take a moment to reflect and look back over your life. Think of the times you quit, gave up, and wanted to throw in the towel. Then begin to thank God, that through your lowest of the lows He remained faithful and brought you through every situation, every obstacle, every trial.

Day 21 - GOD CHOSE YOU

James 1:18 – *"Of his own will begat he us with the word of truth, that we should be a kind of first-fruits of his creatures."*

You did not choose God. God chose you. You did not find God. God found you. God saved and redeemed with His own blood of His own will. He chose YOU! And God is not fickle. That means He doesn't choose you one week and un-choose you the next. He doesn't save you one month and then un-save you the next. He is too faithful to operate in a manner like that. He chose you to be a kind of first-fruit of His creation.

Creation, by definition, means the proprietorship of the manufacturer. A proprietorship is the owner or person who has the exclusive right to something as real property. If you have ever rented an apartment or a house, then you understand the principle of proprietorship. The proprietor owns the property and is therefore responsible for the care and upkeep of the property.

Essentially, God not only chose you but He owns you. You may think that sounds somewhat restrictive, but it is actually liberating when you understand proprietorship. You see, when you are renting an apartment, and something breaks or needs fixed, you don't fix it yourself. You call the proprietor, or landlord, tell him what is broke and if he is a faithful landlord, he fixes the issue.

Here's a statement for you: God is not a slum-lord! He is a faithful proprietor who fixes what is His property. You may be facing insur-mountable issues or feel as though everything in your life is breaking. Call your landlord and trust Him to fix it. He owns it. Let Him fix it.

Day 22 - THE MYSTERY REAVEALED

Colossians 1:26-27 – *"The mystery hidden for ages and generations but now revealed to his saints. To them God chose to make known how great among the Gentiles are the riches of the glory of this mystery, which is Christ in you, the hope of glory."*

A mystery, according to scriptural definition, is truth that has been covered up. Mysteries require revelation in order to be understood. Revelation only comes through the Spirit of God as the Lord takes the cover off of scripture and shows that truth to you. The mystery here being described is "Christ in you." This amazing truth is one of the most incredible and uplifting revelations throughout all of humanity. Christ in you! There are many things to be said about this simple phrase, Christ in you. The toughest person to convince that Christ is in you, is YOU. Especially since you know you. How could Christ, the personification or perfection and holiness, live in you? You know all your downfalls, shortcomings, and sinfulness yet for the believer this is still the promise, Christ in you.

The other truth revealed is, what is in Christ is in you. 2 Corinthians 1:20 says "For all the promises of God in him are yea, and in him

Amen, unto the glory of God by us." Look at this, all the promises of God are in Christ and Christ is in you. Not only are the promises of God in you through Christ, but because of Christ, the promises already have a "Yes" attached to them. The promises of God are not "No." God has already put a Yes on His promises because of the work of Christ in the death, burial, and resurrection.

The fact that God's promises are in Christ and Christ is in you also now reveals why we also have the hope of glory. Through Christ and the promises of God, you always have hope. Be encouraged and let this mystery be revealed in your spirit.

Day 23 - THE WORD

John 1:1 *"In the beginning was the word..."*

God has always worked through His Word. When God wanted to create light, He used His Word. When He wanted to create vegetation on land, He used His Word. When He healed, He sent His Word. When He sent salvation to mankind, He sent THE Word.

Not only has God always worked through His Word in the past but He still currently works through His Word.

God releases His Word through His people and God has given you the authority and dominion to speak His Word by faith and believe that it will produce results.

Life and Death are in the power of your tongue, (Proverbs 18:21) but what comes out of your mouth is a result of what is in your heart. Jesus said out of the abundance of the heart, your mouth will speak. When you vocalize what is internalized then you will see it materialize!

Begin to align your confession and decree with God's Word and believe that it will begin to materialize.

Day 24 - YOU HAVE THE SAME SPIRIT

Romans 8:11 - *"If the Spirit of Him who raised Jesus from the dead dwells in you, He who raised Christ Jesus from the dead will also give life to your mortal bodies through His Spirit who dwells in you."*

As you have read this scripture, I want you to make this declaration: "I have the SAME resurrection Spirit of Jesus Christ living in me!" The spiritual truth being revealed today is that you have the same Spirit. God gave you the same resurrection Spirit when you were saved, born again, and filled with the Holy Spirit. He didn't give you a counterfeit or generic off brand Spirit. He gave you the real thing.

Somehow along the way, Christians have come to believe that they receive a lesser or "not quite the same" Spirit. The analogy being: if you want a hot fresh pizza from your favorite pizza place then you would not go your local grocery store and buy an off-brand pizza from the frozen section. That frozen pizza has a different spirit in it. You want the real thing, not something that is close or good enough.

It is the same principal when you received the Holy Spirit into your life. You did not receive a different Spirit. Rather, you received the SAME Spirit that dwelt in Christ. Think about it, the same dead-raising, water-walking, blind and mute man-healing, demon-casting-out Spirit that was in Jesus is also in you.

Jesus said in John 14:12, *"Verily, verily, I say unto you, He that believeth in me, the works that I do shall he do also; and greater works than these shall he do; because I go unto my Father."*

The same works, because you have the same Spirit. Therefore, if you have the same Spirit, you also have the same power, the same authority, the same peace, the same direction, the same nature, the same everything!

Day 25 - CONVICTION AND CONFESSION

1 John 5:4 – *"For whatsoever is born of God overcometh the world: and this is the victory that overcometh the world, even our faith."*

The Bible speaks often of faith and the untapped potential to every believer when faith is activated and acted upon. The Bible also speaks of the seemingly unbelievable and practically impossible accomplishments of those who acted by faith. Hebrews 11:6 declares that it is impossible to please God with it. Faith positions you to overcome.

Faith has two main elements: Conviction and Confession. You have to believe it before you say it. Faith truly has to be in your heart before it comes out of your mouth. Jesus said your mouth speaks from the abundance of your heart. The Apostle Paul wrote in 2 Corinthians 4:13, "I believe and so I speak." When it comes to faith and overcoming, belief and conviction are essential. Here are three reference points to help you focus your faith as you overcome.

1 - Believe in What He Did

Believing in Jesus automatically qualifies you to overcome. Placing your faith in the death, burial, and resurrection of Jesus Christ is always the first step to overcoming.

2 - Believe in What He's Doing

Romans 8:28 – "*And we know that all things work together for good to them that love God, to them who are the called according to His purpose.*" Let your faith and conviction rest in the fact that God is working for your good. It may not seem good, look good, or feel good at the moment, but faith is not about what you see or feel. Faith is about what you know and believe.

3 - Believe in What He Will Do

Proverbs 4:18 – "*But the path of the righteous is like the light of dawn, which shines brighter and brighter until full day.*" God's plan for your life is not for it to get darker and darker but brighter and brighter. You are the Redeemed of the Lord.

According to 2 Corinthians 5:21, you are the righteousness of God in Christ. Let your conviction and confession rest in the God of your salvation and let them lead you to light!

RECHARGE!

7-DAY
FAITH LIFT

RECHARGE!

Day 1 - WHAT IS FAITH

Mark 11:22 – *"And Jesus answering saith unto them, Have faith in God."*

Faith comes from the Greek word "Pistis", which means: Conviction, Confidence, Trust, Belief, Reliance, Trustworthiness, and Persuasion.

Wow, that's a mouthful. I always find it amazing how one word can have so many different meanings, and so it is with the word Faith. Faith is not a feeling. It is not blind assurance. Faith is not an abstract word which stands by itself. Faith, first and foremost, is a Conviction.

Conviction is the state of being Convinced. Convinced in our belief to the point that we are Confident. However, it is not enough just to be convinced and confident. We have to know WHAT we are convinced and confident about. Some people teach to have faith in faith. So does that mean we should have confidence in confidence? I don't think that's possible.

Our conviction and confidence is in Jesus. Confident that He is the Son of God. Confident that He was born of a virgin, suffered on a cruel cross, rose again from the dead, and now He is seated at the right hand of Majesty on High. Confident that His blood still cleanses from unrighteousness. Confident that He still heals, forgives, delivers, saves, and sets free.

That's the message of the Gospel. This confident conviction leads to a total Trust and Reliance on Jesus.

The key is found in 2 Timothy 1:12. Paul wrote *"...for I know whom I have believed, and am persuaded that he is able to keep that which I have committed unto him against that day."*

Being persuaded comes from knowing whom you believe. No wonder Paul wrote, *"that I may know HIM,"* (Philippians 3:10). I want to encourage you to press in to know HIM. When all is said and done, the only thing that really matters is not reputation, good works, or success. But do you know HIM.

Lord help me to press through and press in to know You more and more each day.

Day 2 - THE FIGHT OF FAITH

The writers of scripture, as inspired by the Holy Spirit, were very descriptive in their use of language. Constantly, the word of God is giving us real life, hands on examples to provide a visual and help us learn.

Paul's writing to Timothy is another great example. On two different occasions Paul refers to his walk of faith as a fight. 1 Timothy 6:12 tells us to Fight the good fight of faith, and 2 Timothy 4:7 says that Paul fought a good fight, and kept the faith. Jude 1:3 says it like this, "*Earnestly contend for the faith which was once delivered unto the saints.*" All three descriptions compare our faith walk with a boxing match. Excuse my West Virginia language but, Ain't that the truth?

Many times walking and living by faith seems to be an all-out war. The battle of the ages. Just like Ali versus Foreman. (maybe that analogy puts a date on me, LOL). Paul even told the Corinthian church that he had been knocked down but not destroyed.

We generally don't view ourselves as fighting the fight of faith but many times that's exactly what it is, a Fight! Sometimes you have to fight to keep believing.

The word fight means to contend with an adversary. You will find a common thread to all of our fighting as believers - our adversary, the devil.

Remember, we wrestle not against flesh and blood. It would be much easier if we could just go up to someone and tell them off to fix the issue. But people are not the root of the problem. The real fight is with the spirits that may be influencing them.

If we allow the enemy to turn our attention away from him and onto people, then he's already won. It's a fight of our faith and it must be fought in the Spirit.

Jesus told Peter in Luke 22:31-32 that Satan desired to sift him as wheat but He (Jesus) prayed for him that his (Peter's) faith would not fail. Notice Jesus didn't say He told the devil NO. He prayed that Peter's faith would not fail in the midst of the sifting.

Many times we pray to be taken out of the fight, when Jesus is praying for us to stay in the fight and be strong. You may get discouraged, (we all do sometimes). But encourage yourself in the Lord. You may get weak. Well Praise God, that's when HE is strong. You may get knocked down but get back up and keep fighting. You are armed with the Sword of the

Spirit which is the Word of God. Use your weapon. Keep on fighting. And when it is all over, you can stand like Paul and say, "*I have fought a good fight ...I have kept the faith.*"

Whatever you are facing is only an attack on your faith. Keep the faith. You're going to win. If God be for you, who can be against you?

Be encouraged and have a blessed day in Jesus' Name!

Day 3 –BE STRONG IN FAITH

Romans 4:20 says that Abraham *"staggered not at the promise of God through unbelief; but was strong in faith, giving glory to God."*

'Staggered not' actually means he did not oppose the promise of God through unbelief. Unbelief will oppose your promise, or literally repel the promises of God away from your life. Unbelief sets in when you doubt the ability of God.

But the Bible says that God is able to do exceeding, abundantly, above all we could ask or think. God is able to perform.

Abraham believed in God's ability and stayed strong in faith by giving glory, or Praise, to God.

It's hard to doubt the promise of God when you are continually thanking Him for what He has promised! Giving glory, thanking and praising God for what He has promised will keep your faith strong in seasons where it appears God is not moving.

Stay strong in faith. Keep praising God in advance for what He is going to do and what He has already done!

Day 4 –FAITH IN GOD

Romans 4:21 – *"And being fully persuaded that, what he had promised, he was able also to perform."*

'Fully persuaded' means that Abraham was convinced by faith that God would fulfill the promise to give him and Sarah a son. Faith gives you the evidence of what is not seen. There was no natural or physical reason for Abraham to believe in the promise. Yet, Abraham was fully persuaded, or convinced in the faithfulness of God. He may not have had any physical evidence, but he had the only evidence you need –

God Said So!

Sometimes you just need to look at your situation and declare that you are victorious because God Said So. Tell that sickness you are healed, because God Said So; tell yourself your family will be saved, because God Said So; tell your checkbook it will be blessed and prosperous, because

God Said So!

If God said it, then He is able, powerful and strong enough, to perform exactly what He

135

said. Faith will give you the unlimited potential to trust in God's unlimited power! God is a big God and is about to do something big in your life.

Why?

Because He Said So!

Day 5 –BELIEVING IN FAITH

2 Corinthians 4:13 – *"We having the same spirit of faith, according as it is written, I believed, and therefore have I spoken; we also believe, and therefore speak."*

Faith is reinforced by what you say. We will see with our eyes what we speak because ultimately what we speak is what we believe.

The spirit of faith is not declaring something that deep inside you really do not believe. That would be counter-productive and contrary to God's operation.

The spirit of faith means saying what you believe because what you believe is what you have heard and what you have heard is God's Word! Jesus said in Mark 11:23 that if you believe, you will have whatever you say. The focus here is not so much on what you say as what you believe. Your words simply reinforce what you already believe.

In 1 Kings 18, Elijah heard the sound of abundance of rain and told the people to get ready. His words gave voice to what he heard in the Spirit and he ended up seeing in the natural what he heard in the spirit.

137

Let your words and your faith line up with God's word and believe that God has put His authority in your mouth.

Day 6 –THE SPIRIT OF FAITH

2 Corinthians 4:13a – *"We having the same spirit of faith..."*

Faith is spiritual - not natural - and sees through the Eyes of God. The eyes of God see through the supernatural. Supernatural being that which supersedes or is greater than the natural way of thinking or operating.

Therefore, Faith enables us to look at situations in the natural but see God's supernatural view point instead. That is how the just can live by faith.

The just, or righteous, will see what everyone else sees in the natural but respond the way God responds because they see it through different eyes, supernatural eyes. In the natural, are you looking at impossible situations in your life but still believing by faith and looking through supernatural sight? Great! That means you are expecting by Faith.

For with men (in the natural) this is impossible, but with God (supernatural), ALL things are possible. What you need, you cannot get with men. You can only get it WITH God!

The good news is, If God is for you then who can be against you?

Faith attracts the favor and supernatural working of God to your life. Keep believing because God is faithful to complete what He has started. See it in the Spirit and watch the promise manifest in your life.

Day 7 –THE SOURCE OF FAITH

Romans 10:17 – *"So then faith cometh by hearing, and hearing by the word of God."*

Let's flip that thought for a moment. If Faith comes by hearing the Word of God, then how do you suppose that doubt and unbelief come? Doubt and Unbelief come by hearing whatever is contrary to God's word.

The Bible tells us that God's word is truth. Therefore, whatever is contrary to God's word is a lie. So then faith comes by hearing the truth of God's word, but doubt and unbelief come from hearing a lie.

Doubt comes by hearing a bad doctor report, but faith comes by hearing God's word: by His stripes you are healed. Doubt comes by hearing a bad report about your children, but faith comes by hearing God's word: you and your entire house will be saved.

You have three gates: Ear Gate, Eye Gate, and the Mouth Gate. Two gates are entrances and one gate is an exit. What you take in through the entrance gates will affect what comes out of the exit gate. If God's word is entering through your ear and eye gates, then faith will come out through the mouth gate, or what you say. If doubt and unbelief are entering through your ear and eye gates, then doubt and unbelief will come out of the mouth gate.

Guard your gates. Make sure you are hearing the right thing so you can believe the right thing.